The Once Mighty Midway Revisited

by Irvin F. Cohen

RoseDog ❧ Books

PITTSBURGH, PENNSYLVANIA 15238

RoseDog Books
585 Alpha Drive
Suite 103
Pittsburgh, PA 15238
Visit our website at *www.rosedogbookstore.com*

ISBN: 978-1-4809-6284-2
eISBN: 978-1-4809-6305-4

Contents

Foreword v

Preface xvii

An Epilogue as Prologue xxii

Chapter

  I.   First Impressions 1

  II. Coming of Age 10

 III. A Biker's Bitchin' Badass Bash 16

 IV. A Very Short List of the Greatest Generation's Res Gestae .28

  V. Once More, Dear Friends, Once More Again
Let Us, You and I, Behold The Very Worst 38

 VI. Yet Still More Bad Vibes Rising 48

 VII. But For Now, Let Us You and I, Dear Readers
Let Us Sing a Paean to Our Heritage
And Sadly Slowly Fading Fast, Distant Memory 61

VIII. Yet Still More Cause For Bitchin' 'n Moanin' 73

 IX. Yet More Sorrowful and Lamentable Professions
of Buyer's Remorseful Confessions .83

  X. And Finally Some Last Rites and Other Pronouncements .101

Foreword

I am a lifelong, intellectual, philosophic, polemical and ideological conservative. No Johnny-come-lately "neo-con" am I. Furthermore I am thoroughly unabashed and unapologetic, for I am one who absolutely makes no pretenses whatsoever, nor apologies nor excuses for my conservatism - nor do I see any reason why I ought, should or must.

But I am also a lifelong conservative voice crying out in the wilderness; and ofttimes an uncannily accurate but tragic Cassandra-like figure who goes unheard and unheeded; and who thusly toils and labors anonymously in the desiccated vineyards of anonymity.

That is until recently, when I discovered the internet roughly three years ago. Since then I have posted and have had roughly one article, essay, satire and or poem published therein per week. Unfortunately it has not been a very happy or benign experience for me, although I must admit and confess that it has been one helluva an intense, learning experience.

What I have learned is that the internet is not a bastion of enlightenment, cultivation and intellectual freedom. But rather it is a refuge of shallow anti-intellectualism, censorship and knee jerk, petty biases and prejudices. It is in essence a New Age, barren moonscape of group think and conformism which sadly pays hollow lip service to bonafide and legitimate, unfettered, free-wheeling and dealing, rigorous and open debate; and sadly, a place where reasonable, rational and honest dissent is barely if not tolerated at all.

I have been censored, shouted down and smeared and assaulted with the most vicious and vile ad hominem attack imaginable. Not only have many of my posts and comments been emended, but literally tens of my articles have been deleted outright; and literally hundreds upon hundreds of my comments and the comments of visitors to my own threads and the threads of others, have either been emended, expurgated and cut into shreds of nothingness, or just simply deleted in their entirety. (I.e., many of these editors simply destroyed the evidence, which of course, is a typical form of intellectual and philosophic fascism.)

(As I stated before, I am rather new to the internet and computer technology, so it took me a little while to learn how to keep a reasonable account of these. So I can't say for any certainty how many of these were either emended, expurgated and or deleted prior to that point in time. But as I recall it was a considerable number. Moreover, of those which I did manage to record, of the two categories, those of my own comments and those of others, in each category was at least two hundred plus in number.)

However to be brutally honest, I must admit and confess to the following irony: not one conservative site was interested in publishing my articles and many of the former just simply ignored me. Yet several of the usual suspect, commie-lib, lefty, pinko and Darwinian-socialist, true believer, fanatical pro-totalitarian fascists and scientific and secular extremist sites - did.

To be sure, even though the latter sites initially welcomed me, they also eventually turned on me, massively censored and then ultimately banned me entirely from their sites. Well so much so for intellectual freedom and open and honest debate on the internet amongst the usual suspects. I.e., again: the commie-symp, commie-lib, commie-loving, lefty-pinko, socialist and commie, Neo and New Age Marxists on the one hand; and on the other, the libber-teen, secular extremist, Darwinian socialists; all of whom also share pro-totalitarian, police state, collectivist true-believer, fanatical, fascistic ideologies as well.

Incredibly they all declaim egalitarianism as their goal and intellectual lifeblood, yet at the same time consider themselves to be elite "philosopher princes" who must be honored, respected and heeded - or else. It is a tyranny of Marxist and Darwinian-socialist, intellectual elitism which can and has been very aptly and accurately described by George Orwell:

> "All animals are equal, but some animals are more equal than others."

ii

Unfortunately it is my rather pessimistic observation and opinion that we are now perilously closing in upon a triumphant, counter-cultural, Marxist-driven, prophetic moment; one which is also in the process of auguring in a New Dark Age of Unreason, ignorance and anti-intellectualism, and one which I envision will also be unpropitiously requited and filled with dystopian chaos and anarchy.

And each day sees us further sinking into this quicksand morass of true believer, fanatical, feudal socialist, police-state totalitarianism: submerging ever deeper into this sinkhole and bottomless pit of solipsism and narcissism with its utter tyranny of radical individualism, self-realization and self-actualization; and again, further into the abyss of shallow and superficial intellectualism, massive anti-intellectualism and monumental ignorance.

And so even Shakespeare's Mark Antony is more prescient and prophetic than he could have ever imagined when he says:

"Oh Judgement! thou art fled to brutish beasts,
And men have lost their reason."

Yes, I recognize and maintain that we live in a New Age, in fact, to be more fully accurate and precise; we are now upon the very cusp of a New Dark Age of Unreason, of massive ignorance, highly conformist group think, and utter intellectual and cultural barbarism. And this Brave New World of "fundamental transformation" is one in which "change" for the sake of "change" is more valued than the lessons of the Classics and the Great Books and the Heritage of the Ages contained within them.

And yes I also recognize and admit that I might represent and could actually be part of that last vestige of both intellectual cultivation and literacy, as well as traditionalism, conservatism and objective rationality. And as such I also recognize and fear that I might just be the last dying gasp of a dying breed. I might not be able to "turn out the lights" on my way out, but out they will be - of this I am certain.

But it is much more than just traditionalism, conservatism and objective rationality which compels and drives me so very greatly. It is also a deep and profound, all-consuming passion and all-abiding love for knowledge, wisdom and ultimate truth: for human progress, enlightenment and the advancement of civilization; for rationality and objectivity and the shared values of good ole middle class, bourgeois, common morality, and common sense, and common decency; and above all else, for personal and individual, intellectual accountability, honesty and integrity.

Lamentably, I see all these ages-old, noble virtues quickly slipping away in a roiling sea of moral and cultural relativism where there is no such thing as clear and lucid, objective truth and reality: where Machiavellian "might makes right" is the eternal, central theme and mantra, siren call of the usual suspects; wherein they unctuously and deceitfully impose their fascistic, political correctness and multi-cultural diversity-doggerel upon all; and where the former casuistically argue their obscurantist sophistry, wherein they selectively choose and manufacture their own morality; and again, impose it upon all of society and its institutions, both private and public, civic-minded and governmental.

All of which I maintain is done to the utter detriment and exclusion of all those time-honored traditional civic and private institutions which have served our nation so well throughout our brief history and which have truly made us both exceptional and so very unique and great. So I therefore must ask, nay, I must demand, where is the personal and individual integrity and honesty of these IT usual suspects, where is their virtue, their ethics, their tolerance of others - other than nowhere to be found? Have they no shame, no honor, no manly virtue? No common decency? No human empathy, no humanity?

Again, ole Shakey's got this one right:

> "The abuse of greatness is when it disjoins
> Remorse from power."

Allow me to interpret this more broadly than it's original context. Of course ole Shakey is speaking of the innate and inherent nature of power, of how it ultimately corrupts us by stripping us of our own empathy and humanity. Well, as I see it, we live in an age where all our very clever and extraordinarily smart technology; without moral instruction, without the tempering of the soul by the lessons, again, of the Classics and the Great Books and the Heritage of the ages contained within them; sadly results in a diminution and abandonment of our empathy and humanity, and ultimately, of our very souls.

It makes us slaves to the dictates of moral and cultural relativism, and to the tyranny of soulless, remorseless experts who do not feel the least bit restrained nor inhibited in exercising and abusing their vast powers, and thusly in ultimately denying us of our very own empathy and humanity, as little and as meager as that might be in this day and age.

Yes, I readily admit that we live in a new age, in fact and indeed, I maintain for the umpteenth time, a New Dark Age of Unreason, one of monumental ignorance and of massive, cultural and intellectual barbarism. But I also recognize and understand that change is constant, that it is always with us, in fact with every passing generation; and that indeed, change is ultimately inexorable, inevitable and ineluctable. Or as the pre-Socratic philosophers were wont to state it, panta rei literally, its word-for-word translation - "all things flow"; or as it has evolved in the past two plus millennia, all things are in flux (or constant motion); i.e., simply put, all things change. End of argument, end of debate.

But there is change and there is change. That is to say, not all change is for the better. And mindless change, change purely for the sake of change, is more often than not, usually for the worse; and moreover, is also usually quite dangerous and thoroughly destructive and evil.

Furthermore, as I see it, there is also a pattern in this change, for although change might be a constant, it is not always linear. In fact, far from it. As I see it, it's always two steps forward and one backward, and vice-a-versa, and a whole bunch of combinations in between therein, thereof. But there is no denying that the most recent trend in this process is to repeat itself with greater frequency and intensity, speed and dynamism.

So yes, I must confess and admit that I bitch and moan about this and that particular, mindless change, like a typical old fuddy-duddy, unhip geezer - but believe it or not, that's not my purpose. Rather, my purpose herein is to critically and analytically chronicle, encapsulate and summarize, what I have both witnessed personally, and what I have observed and formally studied of civilization and of the human condition for the past 60 years of my life.

I only hope that I have learned well and will be able to pass on whatever little wisdom I might possess, to these new and many, subsequent generations. However, whether I succeed or not, dear readers, is no longer within my own hands and grasp, for that is now totally and thoroughly within yours.

iv

Again, for the umpteenth time, we are now in a period of intense and constant, dynamic change, most of which I find wanting and fraught with great danger; and of which I surely still view as a means and grounds for massive abuse and tyranny. Which I suppose is de rigueur, and is simply to be expected of me. But please indulge me dear readers, just this one nostalgic reprise into my past.

Fifty years ago (in fact, this September of 2013 to be precise) I had the good fortune to learn a lifetime lesson from a lowly, but well dressed, graduate teaching assistant. Why do I mention the state of his attire? Because in that Paleolithic Age of American higher education, a suit and tie for men, and a respectable dress for women, was considered a sine qua non requirement - but again why? Because it showed that education, especially at the university level, was a very serious matter and had to be taken quite seriously, even for college freshmen and graduate, teaching flunkies and slaveys.

His name was Mr. Peck and he came from a fairly prestigious institution of higher learning in Ohio, and unfortunately that's all I personally remember of him. However I still recall what he said for even though it didn't sink in right away (I must confess that I am usually rather slow on the uptake, but not always), it did eventually make sense and greatly influenced me within another ten or so years. It slowly but magically spurred me on and got me to thinking and eventually helped me to connect the dots.

So what did he say already? Well, simply stated: it was his contention that the advent of the telephone, the primary source, then closely followed by radio and especially television; had essentially destroyed "letter-writing" as a literary art-form, one which had contributed greatly to the very high level of literacy in America, indeed for centuries up to that point in time.

Of course, as an aspiring professor of English, his major concern was with the state of literature and culture. But he also implied that good letter-writing was also necessary as a "lingua franca" of all intellectual intercourse within all of society, whether it be business or medicine or law or commerce or culture, both high and low, or any other aspect of human, intellectual activity.

My first impression of his theses and of him personally; was that he was just another academic "flake" mouthing his typical academic, rather meaningless and narrow pet theories. As far as I was concerned he was just another liberal, typical luddite, asserting his fifteen-minutes' claim to fame.

Boy was I wrong. As I previously said, it took me another ten years to truly begin to understand and fathom his ideas and their implications, more clearly and fully. What in essence he had said was that with every quantum leap in science and technology, there comes a corresponding and corollary diminution in both certain aspects of human, sensory perception and in the obsoletization and entire replacement of various forms of lower technologies as a result of that process.

Again, to re-iterate and re-emphasize Mr. Peck's point, it was his contention that first the telephone, then radio and finally television, had destroyed the art of letter-writing in America; and as a consequence of this, our culture and literacy were also adversely affected. A thesis with which I of course tend to agree rather strongly.

But I go a step further for I also see a corresponding diminution in traditional values, that is to say, in traditional morality and ethics as well. It's not just the culture which is debased and coarsened, but it is also our moral and ethical compass and individual, personal integrity which is lessened and diminished as well.

All scientific and technological change brings with itself, its own benefits and disadvantages; its own pluses and minuses. Simply stated, for every gain their is a loss. But for every loss, there is also a complimentary, compensatory and corresponding gain. Yes, for every intellectual and cultural gain there is a corollary loss. But there is also a corresponding compensation in our collective intellects, culture, civilization and even physical being.

So, before phonetic, alphabetic writing came into existence, there was orality, which was based and dependent upon rote memorization mostly through formulaic poetry and poetic story-telling. Modern, phonetic, alphabetic writing and language freed up the mind to philosophic and empirical speculation and abstraction on a massive scale, which in turn opened up the mind to infinite reason, rationalization, logic, empiricism and scientific thought, as well as to art and literature, history and psychology, etc. However it came at a steep cost, for memory has been steadily diminished amongst humankind ever since. But the reward has been modernity and the promise of a future with a steady advancement in civilization and human progress.

Or allow me to phrase it thusly (so that even an IT, secular extremist, so-called, supposed scientific, Darwinian-socialist; geek, dweeb, nerd, dork; might understand): Simply stated, all change engenders its own specific set of corresponding changes. When viewed through the evolutionary process, change is the result of environmental stimuli in combination with genetic mutation which taken as a whole is a matter of scientific, physiological autogenesis. However in the Darwinian scheme of things, change literally requires eons of years, and in fact is measured in increments of tens and hundreds of thousands of years, and even in millions of years.

I maintain that is not the case for evolutionary change in the realm of culture, society, socialization, human intellectual-intercourse and discourse, and the advancement of civilization and human progress. As I see it, the former is a matter of LaMarckian evolutionary biology, in which this sort of intellectual, social and cultural change is measured in terms of thousands, then hundreds of years, and ultimately in mere generations - in fact, in as little as two to three, and many of these, because of the velocity of change, have been compressed in half so that this sort of change now occurs in fifty years or less.

My main point here is that the speed and velocity, and the dynamism and momentum of change has now far surpassed and transcended beyond human ken and cognition; that is to say, it has far surpassed the ability and capacity of humankind to fathom and understand, and to implement and employ it both wisely and judiciously. And I strongly maintain that this happenstance is perilously dangerous; especially as it relates to transformational change and the growing diminution of traditional morality and ethical behavior; as well as individual and personal, autonomy and human empathy, intellectual integrity and honesty, responsibility and accountability, logic and rationality.

I maintain that we are currently at a critical juncture in human development, that we are in the cusp of going from a world of geometric progression to one of an "exponential progression." The leap from "arithmetic" to geometric progression spanned millennia and indeed was vast and quantum in nature. Well, so too will the leap from geometric to exponential progression be, but this leap will be vaster and even more quantum.

Again, in Darwinian terms, cognition and the creation of knowledge was both limited and painfully, glacier slow. In Lamarckian terms, what began as arithmetic progression quickly became geometric in nature and is now on the verge of becoming exponential. The means of measuring this tide in human cognition and sapience is the speed and velocity in which knowledge doubles.

In Lamarckian terms knowledge doubled at first in millennia, i.e., arithmetically; and then in centuries and generations, i.e., geometrically; and now knowledge is doubling in less then decades, in fact it is currently doubling every two years, i.e., exponentially. Moreover, I maintain the speed and velocity of this doubling of knowledge creates and builds its own momentum. So as I see it, knowledge will double in ever decreasing increments so that it will soon double in months, then weeks, days, hours, minutes and even in seconds and nano-seconds.

In fact, I speculate that knowledge will eventually double at a rate greater than the speed of light and hence beyond time itself, which of course is the stuff of pure "science-fiction" - at this moment in time. Moreover, such an occurrence would tend to make the human species superfluous and unnecessary (beginning with artificial intelligence which I maintain is just right around the corner).

If and when artificial intelligence occurs, in order for the human species to survive and compete, it would have to adapt to that new environment, but the adaptation process would be so radical and intensely transformative that the human species as we know it would no longer be recognizable - not even remotely so. As for the particulars, that is just too far beyond the scope of this foreword - just suffice it to say, it represents a new physics, the speed of light, nano-technology and bio-engineering and stuff I haven't yet begun to dream of.

Or as ole Shakey put it,

> "There are more things in heaven and earth, Horatio,
> Than are dreamt of in your philosophy."

v

Yes indeed, in the overall mega, macro, cosmic scheme of things, the long term future might be an inexorable and ineluctable struggle for the very existence of the human species as we know it - whether it will survive or not, and in what physiological form or shape, and whether it will be recognizable as human or not - but what else is new "under the sun?"

However that does not mean we must surrender and just give up the present and near term future - no matter how dour and pessimistic my "sci-fi" speculation and predictions might appear. In fact, as I see it, we have a moral imperative and duty to address and fully deal with these very difficult issues which now currently confront us. We cannot, nor should not, nor must not run away from them; but again must recognize that we have a moral compulsion, that we are morally compelled to face them and address them both seriously and sincerely, and virtuously, vigorously and whole-heartedly. And might I add, resolve them both wisely and judiciously, and more than morally adequately.

Sincerely Yours,

Irvin F. Cohen
27 September 2013

Preface

"The Once, Mighty Midway Revisited" is an epic, poetic journey into the soul of America. It is a serious pilgrimage. No self-indulgent, super-sensitive, narcissistic, shallow and superficial journey of minimalist and dilettante, highly self-introspective and self-absorbed fluff - this poem be.

Unfortunately, as you can clearly see, I'm not very good at this sort of thing - of writing forewords and prefaces, critiques and blurbs and the such. In fact, when it comes to self-promotion; of leading my own parade and or beating my own drum, I actually find all that sort of stuff to be quite distasteful and intellectually repugnant.

However, as I understand, there are several things which are expected and required in the writing game, one of which is the writing of prefaces; and within this arena, one is supposed to say something about the subject but not to say too much, especially something specific; and also no quotes, for such a thing is considered to be rather bad form, like speaking ill of the dead at their own funerals; but rather just saying some indeterminate vagary in order to whet the appetite is quite acceptable and in perfectly good form. Well, all this obviously just ain't my thing.

And then there is the unwritten law, actually custom, to say why one writes at all, and why one wrote this particular poem or book, or why on this or that particular subject. And who or what inspired one to write this work in the first place as well as to acknowledge this or that person or institution. You know - to give a long, thoroughly, self-absorbed, egoistical dissertation into the "ego, liddle ole id, moi, me, myself and I" sort of speech heard so often, in fact, regurgitated ad nauseam, at an Oscars' Awards presentation and the like.

Well, I confess, I write for one reason and one reason only - yes, I honestly admit that my sole purpose and motivation, the true reason why I write, especially poetry - is so that I can go on the "Johnny Carson Show." That's it. Word. Really. Straight up. Um, yah know. And that's the "freaking" flippant truth. Word. Really. Um, yah know whadd ahm sayin'?

But nevertheless, allow me dear readers to make my pitiful and worthless attempt at the former.

Just suffice it to say that the "The Once Mighty, Midway Revisited" is a metaphor of the decline of America through the concerted and steady efforts of the extreme, American-left to subvert and willfully destroy every facet of our civil society and its traditions, and ultimately the entirety of American civilization itself. The epic begins over sixty years ago at a carnival side-show and continues to the present.

It is actually short by traditional standards but at 12,000 (plus) words, it unfortunately, by current intellectual standards, is leviathan and interminable. Nevertheless, it is quite metrical and consequently a quick read, perhaps an hour or two. And of course, I maintain, is well worth the effort.

As for rhyme, meter and poetic schemata and their rhetorical and quasi-technical terms - simply stated - fuck 'em. Yeah, yeah, that's rather flip of me. But I write poetry for two entities: for myself, first and foremost; and secondly for posterity, God and nature and yes, for the future with its promise of immortality. Whether I and my poesy are worthy of the latter is beyond my reach and grasp. That determination, dear readers, is solely yours and that of the vicissitudes of time.

As for my poetry, at first blush it might appear to be the stuff of pure free verse and free association. That is to say, there ain't no "rhyme nor reason" there; no scheme, no acceptable technique nor pattern, no "a" nor "b" nor "c" nor "d" therein, thereat.

Well, I say au contraire. What might appear at first glance to be quite chaotic and disorganized, disordered and even jumbled; if one examines it more closely, one will see that it is actually quite ordered, well thought out and with great design and purpose. Again, I do not write mindless, narcissistic fluff, but rather I deal with ideas, meaningful, powerful and purposeful, thought-provoking ideation.

Moreover, I write mostly in spondees, trochees and iambs in iambic pentameter and some dactylic hexameter here and there. But many of the former are split into two or more lines which gives it an appearance of disjointed and chaotic fragmenta. Or equally as well, much of the former can easily be described as falling within the domain of "free verse" and "enjambement" both of which I must boldly and passionately declare I lustfully adore. However I again maintain that there truly is more rhyme and reason to all this seeming madness and chaos than meets the eye at first glance.

Just one last point. I have both written and studied literature and literary criticism and theory all my life and I have concluded that all of that post modernist, deconstructionist opacity and maddening obscurantism is simply a feckless distraction which inhibits my creativity and paralyzes the entire writing process itself. I really do not need to appease, nor write for, nor serve the dictates of the Marxist clowns who populate and so very much dominate the MLA (the Modern Language Association [of America]).

And again, to put it in rather crude and coarse language - fuck them. Fuck them and the horses they rode in upon; and to belabor the point

- you know that in my inimitably superfluous way, I am quite well known to beat a dead horse so far beyond recognition, that in fact, it is rendered into salami - but to continue the imprecation herein, fuck them and not only the horses they rode in upon, but also fuck them and their cows and pigs and goats and dogs and cats, and their pet piranhas and iguanas too. Let there be no fucking quarter given for, nor prisoners taken of these post modernist, deconstructionist assholes. There, I said it! Have at me if you will.

However, dear readers, if you will kindly indulge me this one, very last point - I promise, I swear, I solemnly pledge, cross my fingers and hope to die - well, wait a minute and whoa there pahdner, perhaps that's a bit too hasty and goes a bit too far - even for me. At any rate, if you think I'm a goddamn hypocrite and have lied, well, fucking sue me.

But again, enough flippancy. Please allow me to answer the legitimate question of why I write, and why I write poetry in particular. My reasons are quite straightforward: I write poetry because it comes naturally to me; because I like it; because it sets my entire being and soul on fire. And yet again, I must re-emphasize and re-iterate the point; because it makes me come alive; because for the umpteenth time, it breathes life and fire into my very heart and soul; because poetry is my very essence and being.

Moreover it is a magical, mystical and mysterious process which again seizes and inspires me inexplicably and thoroughly so; and then flows from my brain and courses through my arteries, veins and capillaries to the very ends of my fingertips. And therein, again, magically, mystically and mysteriously explodes throughout my soul and heart, and ultimately to my pen; and finally onto paper in a timeless abeyance of consciousness; and then finally from whence, to my computer.

Well, that's the inspiration element of the equation, but then comes the perspiration part and there's lots and lots of that. In fact, the inspiration component is the easy part, it just naturally comes out of nowhere and appears magically and inexplicably; it's the perspiration part that's truly hard work, and again, there's lots and lots of it. In fact, more than I could ever wish for or desire.

Yet nevertheless, yes, I readily confess and admit that I have been quite flippant and crude within the confines of this forward and preface - but I have also been just as serious, and perhaps even profound as well. Which I suppose is something you, my dear readers, must choose to accept and tolerate, or choose to reject and not tolerate.

Or as the French might say of me "il fait partie de son caractère."

And so I humbly ask you, dear readers, to read my little epic poem and allow it to determine your choice based upon its own merits, or its lack thereof. At any rate, I truly hope that you will enjoy its rhythm and meter, its rhyme and reason, its design and purpose; and especially so, that you will appreciate its ideas, its vision, its insights, its social commentary and polemical analysis; and that you will happily be swayed and moved by all of the former - just as I have been.

An Epilogue as Prologue

or as ole Shakey slyly said in the <u>Tempest</u>
"What's past is prologue."

<u>The Once, Mighty Midway Revisited</u>, again, is an epic poem in the American tradition; and as such is as accurate a depiction of the American experience to date, as best as I can render it. It in essence is a poetic metaphor of America of the past 60 years as I have so personally and intimately viewed it, and is also a vision of both its present and its future. But it is also a disquieting warning and call for alarm to an America at a crossroads, at a truly, very critical juncture of our very own existence as both a nation and as an idea. Both of which latter attributes and conditions (our existential nationhood and our intellectual, philosophic and spiritual existence) I consider to be amongst (if not themselves) the very greatest ideas and highest ideals in the history of civilization.

However, I regrettably and forlornly see America in great danger; the very same America I love and have literally shed my very own blood for on the field of battle in Vietnam, and for which I am still so very prepared and willing to pay the ultimate price with my own life if necessary - I say again, is in great danger. But what is so very troubling to me is that the threat to America is not so much from without as it is from within - that it is moral decay and dissolution, spiritual, philosophic and intellectual rot and corruption which are our deadliest enemies, and they are all, dear readers, predominantly from within. So this small epic poem of mine is both a clarion call to that danger and a call to arms to combat and defeat that deadly and lethal cancer from within.

But <u>The Once, Mighty Midway Revisited</u> is also a work of art. So please enjoy its language, its metaphor, its imagery, its style, alliteration and rhyme, its meter and cadence. Moreover I strongly wish to point out here, that even though English is my mother tongue and native language, when it comes to the convention of prosody in general, and the rules and schemata of prosody in particular of the English language, I blushingly and very abashedly admit and readily confess great ignorance.

Simply stated, I don't care to waste my time nor concern myself with petty rules and regulations and or with tedious, schoolboy exercises; or more accurately, with the highly pedantic, overly academic and scholastic, convoluted, turgidly intricate and overly complex and sophisticated and nuanced analysis of this or that line or couplet or poetic scheme.

My first and foremost concern is with art: with its style, imagery and metaphor, with the creation of a decent and alluring and appealing, provocative and evocative, well-turned phrase or line or two; and with rendering these into powerfully thought-engendering and vision-inducing tableaus just as a plastic artist might render his or her vision upon his or her canvases.

But of course as one ought, should and must conclude for oneself after having read this small epic poem of mine; that obviously and evidently, message and content are also of very great meaning and concern to me; that I purposefully strive to see to it that my art must also be meaningful, persuasive and appeal to both the mind and psyche, and ultimately to the soul; but in addition, must also appeal to reason and logic, rationality and clear, objective truth as well.

Yet nevertheless, I must again re-iterate and re-emphasize the point, my concern is not at all with detail, process and analysis, but rather my concern is solely with the creative process and the creative act itself (here in particular, the writing and creation of poetry). But also evidently, with great ideas. And once there within that lofty and uplifting empyrean, divine, magical land, that elusive realm and province of great ideas; my next and ultimate desire, is to seek the Platonic goal and ideal of attaining first knowledge, then wisdom, and then ultimately - absolute, ultimate truth. Big, rather tall order. *Ne c'est pas?* Yeah, I think so. Well then, I guess I'll just stick with a well-turned and evocative phrase here and there.

Just one last word on my poesy - I am a Classicist by training, choice and personal advocation and predilection, and as such have always been enamored of Homer and the Greek, Lyrical poets - but my greatest love and admiration is for Homer and in particular, for his Grand Style - i.e., for Homeric dactylic hexameter. However, I of course must admit and confess that as much as I have striven to capture that most exalted, style and very great artistry, again in particular, with the Grand Style with its Homeric dactylic hexameter; I must confess and admit that I have been spectacularly and decidedly unsuccessful in that noble goal and quest of mine.

The point is Homer is a great poet, in fact, as far as I am concerned there are only but two poets in all of creation: The two are Homer, who, in me umble estee-mation, is the greatest poet of all time; and Shakespeare, who again in me umble estee-mation, is a close second. After these two, all others are second and third rate and worse. Well, I am no Homer and I of course am no Shakespeare either. As for whether I am second or third rate or worse, I shall fondly leave that determination up to you, the reader; and to whatever second and third rate, worthless, scumbag critic, editor and or battened, professorial monks in ivory cloisters, who might read my poesy in the first place; and who even more incredibly, might condescend and deign to comment upon it in the second place.

In addition, although my poetry might at first blush appear to be without design, schemata or discipline, in fact, to be nothing more than wild, undisciplined free-verse, so very maddeningly riddled with "enjambement" and half iambs, spondees and trochees; believe it or not, there is more rhyme and reason, scheme and design, meaning and purpose to my poetry than the reader might at first blush recognize or acknowledge.

Nevertheless, I must readily admit and cede the point that I have not been very successful in my goal of both creating and capturing the least modicum of dactylic hexameter. And yet again I seem at best to come up with a bunch of undisciplined, unplanned, internal rhyme and alliteration, what are called in Classical grammar, usage and style, as absolute constructions; such as the genitive and ablative absolutes found in both Latin and Greek, as well as accusative absolute, double accusatives and the Cognate Accusative which are mostly found in Greek prosody.

All of which is to say, that I clearly possess a rather large if not huge capacity to be a rather boring, pedantic asshole. Which is the point of all this - less analysis and pedantic bullshit, and more creation and doing in its stead. And in fact "doing" is the essence of poetry for the word itself is derived from the Greek root/stem *poie-*, and the infinitive, *poiein*, which literally means "to make, to do (and ultimately) to create". So again, once more, less bullshit and more doing; more spark, more animation, more inspired, aroused and uplifting creation. And all that other jazz too, and I say, "yeah man, yeah."

Chapter I
First Impressions

When I was but a mere child
six plus decades ago
I both admired and feared
the then mighty Midway with its many impresarios
and its hosts of 'carney men'
and unseen multitudes of roustabouts

for they truly were rough-hewn, rough-looking men
so very fear inspiring to me
a mere child then
but nevertheless
I was so very charmed and intrigued
and so very curiously captivated by them

and so with the smell of cotton candy
in my nostrils
and the feel of sawdust, dirt and clay
beneath my feet

I gazed upon them intently,
intently mesmerized by their

discrete promises of unending, limitless exotica
to be oh so cleverly revealed and oh so gratuitously

and as I gazed upon those sincerely
insincere hucksters
and deeply breathed in of their
alluring siren call, I oh so magically heard
their deeply mystical, magical spellbound spiels:

""Gather around me
boys 'n girls
ladies 'n gents
cause this is gonna be

the greatest lil' show
you'll ever see
on this little ole earth of ours,
this solar system's
virtual third planet
from our burning, incandescent eternally hot sun

I guarantee it
and who else
in this dog-eat-dog world of ours
can make such a claim?
and keep that promise too?
and deliver this world up to you

beyond your wildest imaginations
cause brothers 'n sisters
I guarantee it
and brothers 'n sisters
I never lie
never!

trust me

so step right up
and come and see
the only one of this
and the only one of that
and cast your eyes upon

every assorted misfit
and hideous grotesquerie
and odd, human vagary

every "mis" - formed, "mis" - created and deformed aberration
known to humankind and beyond
to our very God and creator
and to the angels who weep for them

cause we've searched
every corner, nook and cranny
of this universe of ours
and gathered and rounded up

the strangest and most bizarre
oddest creatures alive
on the face of this earth of ours
solely for your very own,
personal edification
enlightenment and bemusement

so step right up
my brothers 'n sisters
come thee one and all
boys 'n girls
ladies n' gents

stand before me and lend me your ears,
my good fellow citizens,
and also your minds
and noble, brave hearts
and your ever-lasting, eternal
immortal souls too

and see it all
good people
see it all

so don't be bashful
and don't be shy
but dare to behold
these breathtaking marvels

these hideous freaks and geeks
these spine-tingling, mind-numbing
monstrous monsters
these fantastic, wondrous, incredible,
astounding phenomenons

for only two bits
a mere pittance

so be bold
and don't hesitate
cause it only happens once in a lifetime
for those who dare
to behold

so step right up
and pays your measly pezzuzahs
each and every single one of you
and see it all

see Lapida, the jiggly, jiggling fat lady
why she's so damn fat
it takes two whole plow horses
just to lift her up

And see Gonzo
the very fierce man-eating gorilla
from the deepest, darkest
heart of Africa

And Leonora
the spotted, leopard woman
from the jungles
of the deeply verdant Amazon

And Dingo
the wild man
headhunting cannibal
from Borneo

And Otto the geek
who eats live chickens,
who bites their heads off
with his teeth
then swallows their entrails whole

And Jeremiah
the two-headed, three-armed
freak
with four, forked tongues
who hisses dubious hermeneutics
when he speaks

and there's even more
why folks

you ain't seen nothin' yet

for there's still lots more
freaks and geeks
ensconced in this tent behind me
beyond your wildest imaginations and expectations."""

And from out of their tents and booths
and from within their labyrinth of stalls and tented halls
the pitch men pitched their pitches
and the spielers spieled their spiels

and the magic was palpable and real
as these carney men and women
wove and cast their enthralling magical spells

and the gamers chimed
in syncopated chorus
to their all-nourishing, all-sustaining
goddess Fortuna

"Only a nickel
so tries your luck
cause everyone's a winner

come on boys 'n girls
ladies 'n gents
tries your luck
and spin the wheel of fortune
cause tonight everyone's a winner

only one thin dime
just a single, ten-cent silver sliver
and it'll be all so right
cause everyone's a winner

only two bits
a lowly quarter of a dollar
cause tonight it's so very right on
cause everyone's gonna be a winner

just one small token

to be had
at the altar of
one's own taking and sure-handed grasp
on the ever, so fleeting and elusive
brass ring of life."

and as Octavius Augustus Caesar was so wont
and fond of saying
Bis dat qui cito dat
he who pays quickly
pays (doubly) twice

and to be sure
I saw and witnessed
those legions of suckers and fools
pay their shekels
rather gleefully and quite willingly

as they worshipped at the altar
of their goddess Fortuna
with their nickels and dimes
quarters and dollar bills

and the carney men,
pitchmen and spielers
hawkers and hucksters
and shrewd and clever gamers
raked in their loot

just spare change
but in those days
spare change went
one 'helluva' long way
and gave sustenance

to those men and women
the pariah class,
demimonde of America,
who lived so precariously and vicariously
on the edge of society
both polite and otherwise

and I saw those legions of fools
laugh stoically
and smile benignly
because they all knew
they had all been had

for the carney men and women
knew not to be too greedy
lest they ire the mob
and arouse and stir up their wrath
and bring it crashing down
upon their heads and shoulders

because
it was all good fun
and actually truly
all quite satisfying and enjoyable

cause the freaks and geeks
and the roustabouts
and carney men and women
would fold up their tents

and pick up stakes forthrightly
and not return for yet another year

Chapter II
Coming of Age

But as destiny would have it
I grew older
as is the fate
of all God's creatures
who survive perennially
so stubbornly and persistently
year after year

and so then indeed
when another 20 years
had come and gone
since I had first
set foot and soul upon
the Once Mighty Midway

I did return once more again
as if upon an unintended,
uneventful lark
spurred on by kismet and its magnetic allure

and as the poet troubadour

of that day sang
"the times they are A-changing"
and so they were
and with a very mighty vengeance too

And I?
20 years older
but still the fool
and still a soft touch
and easy mark to boot

for I was still so very much
a guileless, clueless sucker
one of P. T. Barnum's hosts of
(one) "born every minute"
but more so, in actuality and reality
one produced and brought forth every nano-second

yet as intrigued
and as ever curious
as I had ever been

I still marveled
at the show
and was thrilled to my very bones
and to the very depths of my soul

by the myriad sounds and noises,
rhythms and vibrations
and all that intriguing karma
and the cool, twisted jazz of it all

as I still stood in awe so very mesmerized
by its exotic imagery
and the many aromas of that grand show

with its myriad spectacles
as I breathed in deeply
of its air and its riveting atmosphere

and was still yet
so very intoxicated
with its many splendid smells
and its many fascinating sounds and sights

and yes
I readily admit and confess
I still remained
that very same clueless, guileless sucker

still so very enamored
of the "little top" and the "side show"
still a craven
unabashed gull

still an easy mark
for their guile and cunning ploys
their clever ruses and stratagems
and their alluring traps and transparent plots

it was as if
I were still a five year old child once more again
and had neither grown up
nor had learned a damn thing

always the sucker
always the soft touch
ever eternally prey
to those petty
demimonde hustlers and hucksters

but again,
as the poet troubadour
then chimed in and lyricized
"the times they (were) A-changing"
and so they truly were
and verily with a mighty vengeance too

but I,
no longer a mere child
but still young in my manhood
no longer feared those carney men and women
as I once had

for those denizens of the Midway
and the big and little tents and tops
and the big and little side-shows
no longer filled me with fear and trepidation

but rather
it was pity
that filled my soul
and turned my heart
towards them

yet I had to ask myself
was it I who had changed irrevocably
and not they?
and again, what of those damnable daunting times too?
for surely those pariah citizens of the Midway
had not changed at all

for surely it was business as usual for them
as it had always been
for a good century or two
in this world's

truly New World

but once more again, it was also
those dawning, daunting, execrable times too
which had changed
and it seemed
as if all innocence had been lost

and irony of ironies
the once tame, but curious, polite society
which had once
allowed itself to be sheered and fleeced
of its pocket change and small coins
so adroitly and cunningly

now turned upon those clever
carney men and women
who now suddenly became
their baneful quarry and prey
for it was now the spielers, pitchmen and gamers

who needed to be
protected from the crowds
of young ruffians and hooligans
and adolescent thugs
(and budding, yet soon-to-be
cruel and merciless, remorseless
virulent and violent gang-bangers)

and so I witnessed thusly
one dreamy, surreal night
over four decades ago
truly the stuff of perplexing bewilderment
of the truly inexplicable

fated vicissitudes of the destiny of change
with its incredible
turning of the tables
of tradition and normalcy, and the constancy
of the age old social mores imbued and steeped
in common decency and morality

this febrile, burning madness
so rife in cataclysmic times
and so unfathomable and be-puzzling
when tradition is so very much bludgeoned
so mindlessly and so remorselessly
by factitious, revolutionary, counter-cultural change

Chapter III
A Biker's Bitchin' Badass Bash

and as I recall
it was a cool March night
humid and thick with a misty evening's dew
with a heavy moisture in the air
so that the crowds were also
quite small and sparse too

but that did not deter
the bikers
who rolled up on their cycles
like a swarm of angry wasps

intent on mayhem
high on drugs, booze and beer
they set out
to put on a show, their own

and rode down the middle
of the Midway
like malevolent, avenging angels
but no godly, cherubic, loving angels were these

but rather, if they were angels
they were satanic and devilish
were those from God's firmament
who had fallen out of grace
and had gone awry
bent on strife, mischief and discord

for they turned up the sod with their muscular, fat Harleys
and scattered the throngs
and crowds
and small multitudes
who had ventured out
that cold and inclement night

and drove them to their cars
and the sidelines
and to be sure
they scuffled with a few
brave enough to stand their ground

but it was no match
and the bikers dispersed them with a few punches
and with crashing beer bottles too
and malevolent, heavy monkey-wrenches
and thick steel chains and deadly, frightful tire irons
and it was all over in a flash

for it was not they
but the carney men and women
who were their
true targets

for they beat up the men
and terrorized the women
and ran the former down the midway

and pinned the latter against their tents,
booths and stalls therein

but nothing occurs in a vacuum
for Mother Nature abhors the former
and "Mutha" Nature is one hell of a "Mutha"
for the sounds of distant sirens
quickly pierced the heavy moist,
humid night air

and even though it seemed an interminable
endless wait at so crucial a juncture
the long arm of the law
finally didst reach this erstwhile, unlikely battleground

and to be sure
it was the cavalry to the rescue
and just in the nick of time

with tear gas oozing and spreading out
in a sickening, nauseating pall
their batons swaying and flailing
indiscriminately

and the bikers in turn gave their all
and stood tall with macho bravado
in this beginning, desperate skirmish
in this unending battle
of this incipient and inchoate cultural war

for this was just one of many fronts
in this newly created cultural upheaval
with its all-out assault upon traditional middle class,
decency and respectability,
and common morality

and finally the police
and state troopers triumphed
arrested a handful of bikers
and drove the rest off into the abyss of the night
onto the wet and slickened highways

and the crowds also retreated
save for a few of us
who were heartier and more stalwart
in our curiosity and bemusement

again it seemed
so very odd to me
and so very ironic that
those whom I had once upon a time
not so very long ago
had feared so very greatly

were now the very ones
who cringed in the shadows
so very fearful of us straight-laced types
of us regular
and not so regular people

it was as if the world
had gone increasingly insane
and ever maddeningly topsy turvy
as if the earth no longer rotated clockwise
but had thoroughly reversed its course

for now those very same
carney men and women
of the ages
cringed in abject terror
for now those very same men and women

who had once so skillfully and adroitly

picked the pockets
of small change
from the parents of this generation of plenty
as a sheepherder
the burrs and ticks from the fleeces
of his sheep

had become victims in my soul
and I weeped for this nation
as I saw and witnessed
this generation of plenty
chide and chortle those two-bit hucksters
and petty gamesters and hustlers

and my heart wept
as I saw
those motorcycle thugs and ruffians
drive their big 'cycles' and fat 'Harley hogs'
down the middle of the Midway

and through the county, fair grounds
and tear up the rich spring sod
and churn and plow up the fertile brown loam
with their highly muscular, deeply chromed,
mighty Harley hogs

and overturn the gamesters' tables
and the hucksters' podiums
and crash through their tents
and burn, riot and loot
and battle the fair goers
and then the police

and so thusly I pitied
those carney people
those freaks and geeks
those petty hustlers, hucksters and gamers
and those seemingly rough-hewn, rough-looking roustabouts

whom once
not so very long ago
I had so very much feared
and stood in awe of

for the world order
had been irreversibly altered
for the novus ordo seclorum
had just then arrived on steely feet of clay
and gossamer wings of stone and concrete

for once upon a time
not so very long ago
the ferris wheel
had rotated
oh so joyously

in a world of normalcy
and decency
and all that was
abnormal and indecent
hid underground

and oh yes
to be sure
there was plenty of hypocrisy
and social injustice
just beneath the surface
of that joyous world

but there was also
a clear knowledge of right and wrong
and folks did not question
why they had to make
such fine and dogmatic distinctions
between them

between
right and wrong
and good and evil
for what they also knew
was that their moral compass
had to be set upon the former

for they all knew
or certainly
their culture and society,
God and country
told, exhorted and inculcated within
and dictated to them

always to choose that which
was right and good
and socially just
and above all else
true and moral

whether divinely inspired
and God given
or wholly innate and derived autogenously
from within our very own human, autonomous nature

for it was right to choose right
and it was good to pursue the good
for both were morality's

and God's imperative

and surely there was
nothing relative about
right and wrong
or good and evil

and surely truth
was self evident
and not relative

and surely truth
was a given
rooted in divine
testimony and prophesy

for there can only be
one God the Hebrews reasoned
and likewise
there can only be one truth
the Greeks echoed
those, our very wise men and prophets said

and likewise there can only be
one morality
to which the doubters and moral relativists
questioned perversely and queried sophistically
whose morality is it anyway?

to which there is only but one answer
everyone's
otherwise
there is only anarchy and chaos
lawlessness, butchery, and utter barbarity

and or
solely the expedient and selective
self-serving truth
of the moral relativists

who create
their own morality
to suit their own needs
partisan wants and desires
and personal whims and caprices

and so that generation of plenty
fell prey to that very great evil
masquerading as wisdom
called moral relativism

and those moral relativists
sang their siren song:

"morality is simply an artificial
construct of men

therefore,
morality is unnatural
and does not exist

therefore
truth is relative

and therefore
God does not exist
so do as you please

and if it feels good
just do it,

and if it feels better
the more you do it,
then do it some more

do it till your eyes
roll up
and your dicks fall off

for there is no God
and there is no right and wrong
and morality does not exist

so it's alright
to do your own thing
cause
unearned, good self-esteem
and unfettered, limitless freedom

and above all else
the self,
the I, the ego,
me, myself and liddle ole moi
is the only truth that matters."

and so
this generation of plenty
this age of wanton excess and brazen decadence
with its inflated, boundless sense of self-importance
raised on Doctor Spock and Madame Montessori

where personal, individual discipline
and responsibility
were to be avoided at all costs
and corporal punishment
was a cardinal sin

where deferred gratification
and hard work
were banished and exiled
and a world of instantaneous,
self-indulgent satisfaction
arose in its stead

where children and child-rearing became
likened unto the
Mexican proverb,

"to cave into the demands and whims
of a spoiled child
is like feeding a snake"

where thusly millions upon millions
of vipers
were hatched and created
in this psychobabblers' netherworld

with its mindless, solipsistic worship
in craven idolatry
to their false, ersatz gods and goddesses
in their narcissistic, slavish devotion
to their phony prophets of unearned self-esteem

where one chose to reason
and talk the little tykes
into submission
while the other argued to love them unconditionally
into good behavior and 'whole' personhood

and so a generation of excess
was born
which in turn has created two more

in its own image

which is another painful irony
for I too was part
of that generation of plenty
and those thugs and hooligans
at the county fair that night

were my brothers and sisters
and we were all sprung from
the very same loins
who are now universally
celebrated as the
"Greatest Generation" ever

how truly ironic
how truly wondrous and incredible
we who were
the very worst generation
in our nation's history

were yet sprung from the loins
of its very best
just as Commodus was from Marcus Aurelius

Chapter IV
A Very Short List
of the Greatest Generation's Res Gestae

yes
we were indeed
the proud
sons and daughters

and rather highly
pampered and spoiled rotten
mindlessly fêted offspring
of the Greatest Generation ever

who had survived the Great Depression
and defeated and triumphed over
fascist tyranny and totalitarianism
militarism and imperialism

but their many accomplishments
did not end there
for they then in turn
created the Greatest Nation ever

for they subsequently
produced the most powerful,
the most prosperous, wealthiest
most humane and compassionate and altruistic
nation in the history of the world

but it was more than just mere guns and butter
and historically, unprecedented
materialistic plenty, cornucopia and satiety
with its rich bank accounts that
that generation of hardship, turmoil and struggle
engendered and created

it was also
the generation
which repealed the ages old
doctrine of
"Vae Victis"

literally
"woe unto the conquered"
as in horribly, horribly woe unto me

for this generation
brought humanity and civilization
to the world
and instead of grinding our defeated enemies
into the ground

as had been the tradition and custom
of nations time immemorial
literally for thousands of years
since the very dawn of civilization itself

we did the complete opposite

for we lifted them up from the ashes
and revived and resuscitated them
and breathed life into their economies
and gave them the gift of the American Gospel
of liberal, democratic, enlightened capitalism

nor did we burden them with taxes
nor turn them into vassal
tribute-paying, subject states
nor erstwhile, dubious, subjugated allies

but again
we did the complete opposite
of what history demanded of us
and dictated again and again
time immemorial

again!

unprecedented
unheard of
in the long annals of history
because what we did
had never been done before

never
not once
not ever

which made America
truly unique
and above all else
without exception

the most civilized
just and altruistic nation
in the entire history of the world

but that Generation,
the Greatest ever,
did not cease nor desist
from imparting its great largesse
to the world

nor cease
from its additional,
greatest mission
here at home
at our water's edge

but instead looked inward
and saw that the promise of America
that its good reputation and bona fides
our divine, godly American Exceptionalism
had been so very forlornly tarnished

and worse still yet
that it had been compromised
and even worse still yet
had been so very awfully sullied and soiled,
polluted and contaminated

by a deadly cancer
a very stubborn and persistent,
malignant pestilent disease
which had been with us
from our very founding

and oh to be sure

it started out as one
of the cruelest conditions
of mankind ever visited upon
one's fellow man

totally antithetical and inimical
to all free men,
truly an abomination
and utter horror,
that vile evil
called slavery

yet to our great credit
we quickly
(even though to this very day
there are many who say it was glacially slow
in its coming
indeed and in fact too damn slow)

yet even so
we nonetheless ultimately
repealed, banned and outlawed slavery
that utter, monstrous demon
of inhuman servitude,
from our very shores

in an internecine struggle
which spilled more blood
on our soil
than any other war
in our very short history

in fact
more blood
life and limb

than all our other wars
combined

yet we willingly underwent that
bloody paroxysm
to right that wrong and banish that utter evil
from our nation

and surely the costs
were enormous
and rivers of blood did flow
unchecked, unabated and unimpeded

but then
a great opportunity
to resolve and solve
that devilish, demonic problem
was lost

for in its stead
arose yet another evil
almost as cruel and pernicious
as slavery itself

for racism
in the guise of segregation
and 'separate but equal' and 'Jim Crow'
took hold across the land

and so we reverted and resorted
to yet another vile and evil monstrosity
to yet another sordid hypocrisy
and moral abomination

for the nation allowed itself

to become enslaved to
and fall into the trap of
both racism and segregation

both de facto and de jure
and this was surely
yet another blight
upon our good name

but in mighty, righteous opposition
the Greatest Generation ever
stood up to the task
and righted that insidious wrong
and utter evil

and outlawed and banned
the scourge of racism and segregation
and fought the good fight
against it

so that today
in my and their own lifetimes
institutionalized racism and segregation
no longer exist

but this Greatest Generation ever
was still not done
for it still faced one last
great enemy,
one last, lethal existential threat
to all of humanity and civilization

in the guise of international communism
embodied in the former Soviet Union,
truly a most "evil empire"

perhaps arguably worse
than the Nazis and the fascists
who paralleled them,

they who were their contemporaries
and their fellow socialist brethren,
national socialists to be precise,
who were truly just as evil
and on a worldwide global scale as well

however it still remains
that arguably the international communists,
the Stalinists and Maoists
were even worse than the former

yet these too
were overcome and defeated
by the Greatest Generation ever
incredibly without a shot having been fired
nor need be expended

this,
the Greatest Generation ever
not only survived the Great Depression
and singlehandedly won World War II
and defeated Nazism and fascism
and Japanese militarism and imperialism

and not only
created the mightiest,
wealthiest nation
in the history of the world

and not only righted
the wrong of segregation

and the scourge of racism
here at home

but also
won the Cold War too,
in spite of our liberals' many attempts
to lose it from within

which was the very last
crowning glory
to its many triumphs and victories

so that all these
deeds and achievements of theirs
of that Greatest Generation ever,
both those within and without
and those both external and internal

when combined
truly make
the Greatest Generation
truly the Greatest ever

for what
they accomplished
I assure you dear readers
were no small matters
nor piddling, inconsequential achievements

my parents'
generation
literally saved the world
and made it a better place

and also made my own generation's

world even better and greater
than theirs
and exceeded every other generation's
which had preceded them

again,
no small, piddling
inconsequential accomplishment
that

So yes indeed
I unapologetically and proudly
sing my song of praise
to that Generation of
men and women
the Greatest ever

I sing of their arms and struggles
and I sing of their great spirit
and many deeds and exploits
and I find them almost entirely
without blemish or fault

but mostly see them
to be with
good hearts
and possess souls of utter decency
and unselfish altruism

those brave men and women
those unsung heroes
who brought succor and peace
to the world
and social justice here at home

Chapter V
Once More, Dear Friends, Once More Again
Let Us You and I
Behold the Very Worst

And so on that night
at the fairgrounds
not quite yet, fully cognizant to me
I began a long journey
of introspection and doubt

Yes, to be sure
my parents' generation
was truly the "Greatest"
for surely
through their deeds and accomplishments

they had earned
the right to that appellation
and surely were entitled
to that honorific

but what of
my generation?

were we in turn
so quite ironically
truly the worst?

again,
that night
at the fairgrounds
was only the beginning
of a long journey
of introspection, doubt and uncertainty

and equally of critical inquiry and analysis,
indeed, a very truly long odyssey
which has spanned four more decades
and four years now

for I still remember that night
at the fair grounds
but not as vividly as I suppose
I ought

because
let me tell you
pah-d-ners
after 44 years

yesterday
is a lot more distant
and a lot more difficult to recall
and a helluva a lot more yesterday
than it is today

but be that as it may
and be it that I am now
also quite long in the tooth

and regrettably quite decrepit too,
that night might not be as
visible and lucid as it ought

but this one thing
I am certain
that night still
remains indelibly seared into my soul

for it truly was
a harbinger of things yet to come
and I indeed truly felt them
begin in earnest that very night
far more so
than any other point in time
since then

and so that evening
the carney, ferris wheel
of joy, happiness and cheap thrills
rotated in syncopated normalcy
as it had always done

as my generation
that generation of plenty
lit up their joints freely
in brazen defiance of authority
and social convention

and smoked the'r 'boo'
and the'r 'Mary Jane' too
in celebration of wanton excess
and unbridled, uninhibited hedonism

and they smoked and toked

the'r 'jernts'
and breathed deeply in of drugs
and of their self-indulgent, sybaritic pleasures

for they said it was only freedom
which they sought
but Hobbes the philosopher
one of many
throughout the ages

rightfully said
this notion of freedom
as an absolute, absolute;
was nothing more than
an empty justification
for licentiousness and libertinism

and so unmindful
of that lesson
of the wisdom of the ages
they rode that very night

upon a very wild merry-go-round
of mind-altering drugs
and visions
of "strawberry fields forever"

and rode the ever soaring
speeding, mind-numbing
roller coaster
of peyote and LSD

vibrating to the electronic vibrations
of primitive and primordial
rock 'n roll

in an undulating orgy
of mystified, electrified Muzak

burning and swaying
to the acid beat
of that rarified air
where their existence,
their very humanity was all but an illusion

where they turned night
into a twilight limbo,
where neither gods nor goddesses
could no longer reside
nor dare tread

and I saw this
my generation of plenty
silhouetted against
a neon skyline
below a pinball mystified,
mystical, magical Midway

withdraw solipsistically
within themselves
and retreat into a putrid sewer
of unearned self-esteem

and wallow in their own
ever-lasting, interminable
overweening self-love
and intemperate, unrestrained narcissism

and I saw this
my generation of plenty
this generation of excess

retreat defiantly
and reject and refuse

the challenge of its
and every generation's
call to arms,
to common, middle class
decency and respectability

and I saw this
my generation of plenty
abandon its very own
moral center and goodly sanity
and rational aequanimity

and sink into
an abyss of amorality
and into the bitter morass of moral relativism
and wanton excess, hedonism and drugs

and I heard
my lost generation of plenty
sing hymns
of self-righteous indignation

and like spoiled children
in mindless, rageful tantrum
make their non-negotiable demands
and truly believe

that if they only just pouted
and only just held their collective breaths
just long enough,
that their demands would be righteously met

what fools
what insane lunatics
what schemers and dreamers
and crazed ingrates
those youths were

and I heard this
my very own generation of plenty
amid a chorus of confusion
in discordant cacophony

sing their very own gospel of excess
of self-serving hedonism
and self-centered solipsism
and egotistical, purblind
mindless narcissism

and belt out
like true rock 'n rollers
their mantras
of "if it feels good, just do it"

and
"books don't count no more
cause it's only feelings that matter
cause if it feels good
it must be good

and if it's good
then it must be right
and if it's right
then its's got to be
true and just

So ""Fahrenheit 451""

them books
and burn them baby burn
in towering, incendiary infernos

and let these
burning pyres
be our monument
to a glorious New Age of Unreason

for it is now the high season
of our utter contempt for the past
for we find
the life of the mind is evil

and so reason
reading books and thinking
is nothing more to us
than apostasy and high treason

so burn them books
burn 'em
rip out their pages
and pile them high
on the funeral pyre

of Plato's
agan dia-leges-thai
of rigorous discourse
and highly reasoned debate

cause we hate
all that shit,
cause it
don't feel right

so you better hide
you better run
you better go underground
but you just best

get out of the way
cause here we
and our Brave New World come
and with a mighty, irresistible, terrible vengeance
too deep to fathom or possibly understand

to avenge
all your hypocrisy
and evil ways
and all your material
wealth and prosperity"

and I heard this
my own generation of plenty
chant, hymn and sing
their irrational,
siren songs of insanity

and I looked upon the past
and reminisced sadly
with both pity and remorse
for that pitiless, pathetic future
they both embodied and embraced

and I held the present forlornly
in great terror
and sadly concluded
there could be no worthy future

with such as these

Brave New World warriors
and Age of Unreason,
counter-culture Elmer Gantry,
omnipresent, ubiquitous Savonarolas

these intellectual louts and barbarians
then and now present
in every direction

as far as the eye
could possibly see and fathom
and oh how truly tragic
that did then and now portend

Chapter VI
Yet Still More Bad Vibes Rising

for there were persistent
ominous rumors in the air,
quite distant tremors and murmurs
in the high atmosphere,

uneasy rumblings from the depths of the Far East
and surely they bode not well
for a new religion
had arisen there
within a thin and ethereal, mystical witches' lair

for a cult
right out of hell
full of Sturm und Drang
and self-righteous zealotry

was marching across
the world stage
and my generation of plenty
stood in mindless solidarity

with its vast armies of

ignorant, primitive and illiterate
highly gullible and superstitious peasants
armed with AK-47s

mouthing communist dribble
and spouting
warmed over Marxist spittle

and those hosts of puritan,
true-believer
conformist fanatics
with their smiling, cherubic faces

waged armed subversion
and armed aggression
and committed massive repression
and genocide
wherever they dared to tread

and my generation of plenty
found just cause
with those barbarians
and offered them
intellectual and ideological succor and fraternité

for they sympathized with them
and were wholly of like mind
with those wild men
remorseless, relentless barbarians
from the East

who were ever so eager
and so completely armed
with the will
to destroy the old

with bombs and bullets
and fatuous and inane
but highly lethal propaganda
and insane intellectual dictates

and to destroy everything which
stood in their maddened, crazed
blood-lust path
to conquer the world

for their so-called noble ends and goals
of supposed social-justice
and the triumph
of Marxist, historical synthesis

surely did not matter
at all,
not one iota nor one farthing
to those barbarians
and to my generation of plenty

whether they should
bring civilization crashing down
and all of humanity to its very knees
and cause endless rivers of blood to flow
in that very same process

for very quite perversely
they both savored such a solution
with its inevitable outcome
of utter misery, death and destruction

for their mantra-call, common and necessary refrain
of the Marxists then
as it has always been time immemorial,

emphatically writ in both stone and torrential rivers of blood,
was and infinitely still stubbornly remains

"you can't make an omelet
without cracking a few eggs,
and (violently) scrambling them too"

so if millions
must perish and die,
well then,
just simply stated
"that's tough shit" and "c'est la vie" too

and there
ain't no need
to cry
over spilt milk

cause
according to their
liberal-socialist, communist dribble
and warmed over, Marxist spittle

Marx was right
and history and his doomsday's might
are unavoidable and inexorable,
inevitable and ineluctable

for there's
no avoiding the Grim Reaper
nor ole Marx
and his triumph of scientific socialism
and socialist class warfare

and my generation,

that generation of plenty,
bought that nonsense
that utter evil
hook, line and sinker

with neither remorse nor healthy inquiry
nor critical, skeptical analysis
but spawned their own
form of intellectual barbarism

and I saw this,
my generation of plenty
shirk its civic
and moral duties

and refuse to lift
one finger
to defend our very own nation
or those of our allies

and I saw them
waste themselves on drugs
and fornicate gratuitously
in libertine, free, promiscuous sex,
and licentiate hedonism and feminism

and I saw them
flee the nation
or buy phony deferments
lest they serve their nation
in its, our hour of need

and I saw
that generation
with factitious and insincere

phony idealism

make excuses
to hide and justify
their every excess
and myriad loci
of moral abandonment
with its massive depravity

and saw that generation of plenty
with a thousand disparate heads
bark and nip at itself
in a wild frenzy

with foaming muzzles
and with the bared teeth
of countless selfish, balkanized
solipsistic, self-serving, special-interest groups

and soon
those barbarians
were at the gates
from whence they invaded
our colleges and universities

and they took them over
and now those very same maddened barbarians and rabid dogs
who were once upon a time not so very long ago,
at and then quickly within those very same gates,
are the very same insane inmates
who now run that asylum

and thereof, therein
my very own
generation of plenty,

have taken over "the commanding heights"
of the culture too

from whence
they have thoroughly contaminated and polluted it
and therein, thereof have eviscerated, coarsened and eroded
the very moral fiber and fabric
of the nation as well

and they have spawned
in a steady, streaming downbeat, two more
worthless generations
in their own image

of even more brain-washed, uncritical
lemming-like, highly propagandized,
fanatical, conformist
brain-dead, intellectual zombies

who mouth post-modernist,
pablum and refried shit-for-brains,
and deconstructionist
intellectual masturbation

who know nothing
and are monumentally ignorant
but worst of all

allow themselves to be swayed and ruled
by moral relativists
and left-wing sophists
and Marxist propagandizers and proselytizers

by those very same
college and university professors

those battened hens in a coop
those fashionable-chic, Marxist radiclib
idiots, imbeciles, morons and cretins

with a vast shit-load of Ph.Ds
with fancy-sounding dissertation and thesis,
doctoral titles
a city block-and-a-half long

which only proves
their monumental, intellectual vacuity
and utter worthlessness

but yet I
remember quite painfully
that it was not so very long ago

when the world was awash
in barbarism,
when angelic-looking monsters

with cherubic smiling faces
little Nazis in reality,
built pyramids of thousands of heads
and buried the dead

where they stood
or in deep trenches
in genocide
across the Third World

and my generation
stood tall
in grotesque solidarity
with them all

or simply looked idly by,
lest all that unpleasantness
from the East
interrupt their hedonism
and easy lifestyles

and here in America
a new intellectual
cultural, philosophic and ideological
barbarism likewise arose

and it was
a contagion
destructive and deleterious
as that

of the religion
which had arisen
and taken hold
in the far East

and it was
as a storm rising
and as a plague
and as a cancerous pestilence
upon the world stage

which threatened
a return to the Dark Ages
and worse
even to the Stone Age as well

if not literally
certainly figuratively,
metaphorically and spiritually

and this tide
of intellectual barbarism and depravity,
this intellectual storm
of pure evil

came to our shores
and was wholly embraced
by my generation of plenty

and insidiously like an epidemic disease
spread across the land
and contaminated our culture
and polluted our schools
and damnably eviscerated and eroded
the very moral fiber and fabric of the nation

not so very long ago
when my parent's Generation,
the Greatest ever,
lost its collective soul
and our nation's
innocence

and handed it over
to a host of philosophic barbarians
and intellectual louts
and cultural thugs and diversity charlatans
and political hacks and moral relativists

and we all
have suffered

ever so greatly
but yet, oh to be sure,
we have not suffered materially

not a farthing nor an iota
and if anything is true
it is not dearth
which we truly must bear and endure

no, again, it is not
wealth nor prosperity
which eludes us so,
but rather tis spiritual attainment,
completeness and intellectual and philosophic
wholesome wholeness

it's the moral courage
and the manly virtues and integrity
of our forbears
of their fierce independence
and rugged individualism

their spunk
and true grit,
their wisdom and common sense
which are now so alien and derisible and lamentable,
which are now so thoroughly
held in contempt and viciously sneered at

by our oh so, very sophisticated elites
oh so, very elevated, acculturated and cultivated
and oh so very ingrained in the ways of our old European rivals,
those Marxist, misfits and clowns
both abroad and here at home

which elude us all so elusively
and so unkindly and forlornly
and which so lamentably rob and deny us
of our philosophic patrimony

and intellectual destiny and fulfillment

and surely
it is the challenge
of this new millennium
which both frightens and terrifies me

for in this New Age of Unreason
narcissism and unbridled hedonism
and intellectual deception and charlatanism

who is to lead the way?
who is to redeem us
and save us from ourselves
if we go astray?

for the Greatest Generation ever
is now in decline
and dying off quickly
in death's last knell
full embrace

while their progeny
truly the worst generation ever
is in the ascendency

so again
who is to lead
the way
into this next millennium?

certainly not
the usual suspects,
that cast of liberals qua commie-libs qua commies
and Marxist firebrand, fools, lunatics,

idiots, morons, cretins and imbeciles

spouting and mouthing off
their so very quite typical liberal-progressive qua liberal-socialist
qua socialist qua communist dribble
and so very trite and banal, warmed over Marxist spittle

surely and certainly
not that generation of plenty
and their ilk
with their own progeny of hedonism

is it
these New Agers
these slackers
and gen-X-ers
and spoiled-rotten millennials?

these unmanly
panty-waisted
geeks and nerds,
mama's boys all?

and those insatiable,
un-requitable, thoroughly unquenchable
'harpy' extreme feminists too?

all so thoroughly
steeped in self-serving
solipsism and narcissism?

for surely they portend and forebode,
alas,
nothing but ill-fated doom

Chapter VII
But For Now, Let Us, You and I, Dear Readers, Let Us Sing a Paean to Our Heritage And Sadly to Its Slowly Fading Fast, Distant Memory

oh where,
oh where,
America,
are those giants?

who founded
this great nation of ours
who created this beacon,
this city of light
upon a hill

this burning torch of hope
to the world
with its message
of salvation and redemption

of its gospel
of freedom and liberty

born from liberal, democratic
enlightened capitalism

oh where, oh where
are those giants
and the intervening
generations of our other giants

those pioneers and burly
frontiersmen
with "broad shoulders"
and burly attitudes

who both engendered and developed,
refined and improved upon
the Gospel of America
of our liberal, democratic, enlightened capitalism

ever so relentlessly
throughout the ages
one generation after another

who not only brought forth
our great nation
but in the process
also birthed

our great
American Exceptionalism
through our Christianity
and in particular

through Protestant Natural Law
from whence
the rights of man

were born

and from whence
all our laws,
our mighty Declaration of Independence
and most wise Bill of Rights
our self-governance and rule of law
ultimately emanated

and in turn,
from whence
our very own, very unique
founding documents

first, with their so very defiant "Declaration of Independence"
and then with their so very well-argued
and thoughtful "Federalist Papers"

and finally with their 'crowning glory'
their and now our Constitution
with its Articles of Confederation and Bill of Rights

all ultimately derived from
our humanity and human empathy
again, all of which emanated
from our Christianity and in particular
from our American Protestant Natural Law

where are those giants
who once roamed our shores
and hinterlands
who pressed on bravely
and fought back
and ultimately tamed the great wilderness

who spanned the continent
with roads and bridges
and railroads
farms and factories
and created the greatest prosperity and wealth
the world has ever known

where are those giants
where are those generations
of rough-hewn, unlettered men

men chiseled out of granite.
men with chips of stone, concrete and steel
upon their defiant, broad shoulders

where are those
indefatigable, burly men
with their burly attitudes
and their uncompromising
will to succeed

where are those generations
of men of true grit
and destiny
of hope and 'can do' certainty

so very indelibly steeled
within the very innermost recesses
of their hearts and souls

where are those men and women
so intensely tested
branded and marked
by their very own
many trials and tribulations

through those
daunting crucibles of
"blood, sweat and tears"
through which they struggled
and suffered so many unspeakable hardships

but yet ultimately endured and succeeded
and overcame
every hurdle and obstacle
thrown and cast in their way
and placed before them at their every turn

upon their arduous path
in their parlous trek,
in their very much
unending quest for
and ultimate triumph of
freedom, liberty and democracy

where are those
stalwart men and women
who tamed the mighty rivers
and traversed the vast continent

both on foot and by wagon
crossed over the land
and spanned the rugged mountains

who endured
unspeakable, ineffable hardships
yet plowed ever onward
ever, so very resilient, courageous and brave

who dammed
the rivers and lakes

and drained the swamps
and reclaimed the land

who mined the earth
to its very core
and brought forth
mountains of coal and iron ore

and forged
all this bounty
of earthly elements and soil
into mountains of steel

who drilled the earth
to its very core and deepest depths
and brought forth
gushing rivers
and torrents of oil

who with true grit
broad shoulders
and muscled sinew
and burly attitudes

built teeming metropolises
filled with skyscrapers
which reached to the very skies
and challenged and rivaled
the very heavens themselves
who shed their own blood
in the hundreds of thousands
to end slavery
and emancipate the slaves

a deed

again which
was unprecedented
in the annals of history

where are those generations
of giants
true heroes and heroines
brave men and women?

for surely
I lament
their absence

for surely
those great generations
of yesterday and yore
are either dead or dying

moribund
and beyond
the last peel of their, our nation's
perhaps last chance
death's knell's last embrace

and perhaps,
the unkindest cut of all
is that their legacy
will be
so very tainted
by their very own issuance

by our very own current progeny
of perverse boomers
and spoiled, battened 'yuppies'
and worthless slackers

and gen-X-ers and millennials

and by unthinkable,
unfathomable
generations yet to come

of even greater decadence
and moral relativism and personal
moral and ethical dissolution

by those yet to come,
ever increasing
generations thoroughly imbued and immersed
in self-serving narcissism and solipsism
and unending, insatiable hedonism

yet this unholy specter
of even more generations
of spiritual and cultural rot
and philosophic and polemical corruption
and putrid moral bankruptcy
still persists so rather ominously

for will this ironically be
their legacy, their gift
to the endless ages
of remorseless, relentless
time immemorial?

will history be so very unkind
to all of us
with these current ignoble, ignominious
vile generations of shame and disgrace?

or somehow

will history
and future generations
somehow, in some way
manage miraculously to redeem those giants
and brave men and women of yore?

or are we and they
simply doomed
to the trash heap of posterity
and nothing more
than a passing mention

in the Book of the Dead,
a mere footnote
within the many myriad
annals of history

wherein it will say and declare
they had their brief time
upon the stage
of life and history,
their one brief moment

"...full of sound and fury
signifying nothing..."

and they simply blew it, and we'll,
they will all say
"bad luck for them
and I too will ruefully declare
"bad luck for them"
and us
and the rest of the world
and all of humanity too

or will these bums
these slackers
these yuppies and gen-X-ers
and pale, over-stuffed millennials
rise to the occasion?

that is still
of course
a possibility
but certainly their fathers and mothers,
their grandfathers and grandmothers

those boomers
that generation of plenty
my very own
are beyond salvation and or redemption

for the Grim Reaper
daily visits upon them
his grim reward and unwanted gift
of extreme human fragility
with death and ultimate, ineluctable, supreme mortality

in spite of their vain efforts
to maintain their ghostly fleeting youth
and former evanescent being
with their inane, insane desire
to live forever

cause God and Mother Nature
always, always have the last word
in spite of the 'boomers'
overweening hubris
with their vain and laughable attempts to the contrary

cause God and Mother Nature
always, always have the last laugh too
cause the joke is always eternally
upon us mere mortals
whether we 'get it or not'

so what
will it be
America?

a continuation
of the worst
or a new beginning
from those generations
yet to arise

of true conservatism
with its preservation
and continuation
of all that is right and good
just and moral
with America?

for surely
those generations
of giants and brave heroes
with their broad shoulders and burly attitudes
and the will to succeed
are gone
and shall never arise and roam
nor tread upon
this earth
nor grace
this land of ours

so again
what will it be
America?

who will save and redeem us
who will honor, grace and bless us?

or will our future simply be
one of utter, dismal, abject failure
disgrace and ignominy?

which is it
America
what shall it and thee be?

shall we
return to that long, noble line of
generations of giants
who preceded us

or shall we surrender to
these perverse boomers
and their progeny
of moral and spiritual slackers,

un-virtuous and un-resourceful
irresponsible bums and beggars,
and intellectual, philosophic and ideological
louts and lilliputians all?
so once more again
what will it be
America
what will it be?

Chapter VIII
Yet Still More Cause for Bitchin' 'n Moanin'

but I ain't done yet,
folks,
so please
just bear with me
this one last time

and just allow me
dear readers
this one last blast
from the past

for the Once Mighty Midway
to be sure
ain't quite
done and dead
quite yet

for even though
those carney men and women of yore
whom I as a child
first viewed

over 60 years ago

might all be dead and gone now,
true dinosaurs,
and lamentably only a footnote
in the trash heap of time
buried anonymously within the annals of history

perhaps at most
a mere footnote in some
pettifogger's so-called, supposed scholar's
research paper or dissertation/doctoral thesis

truly
the esoteric and arcane work
of second and third-rate monks
in ivory cloisters

who proudly call themselves
anthropologists and sociologists
and puff themselves up
as social, true scientists
and professional scholars

(but know this
and know it quite well
I wince
every time I hear that term
'professional scholar'

because those words are thoroughly
paradoxical and mutually antithetical
and are in complete contradiction
to themselves

for in my mind's eye
the word professional
is thoroughly pejorative
and thoroughly synonymous
with the word prostitute

and scholarship,
true scholarship
is in no way synonymous
with prostitution

but rather is a reflection of
the sum total
of all past thought
and of all intellectual and philosophic inquiry
which is worthy of our study and deep scrutiny

for true scholarship
is truly a noble calling
which constitutes
the very best of man's endeavors

and is surely representative and illustrative
of the very best ideas
of the heritage of the ages
which is a legacy worthy
of our keen pursuit and respect

and above all else,
our fullest intellectual and philosophic
honesty and integrity

and our fullest devotion
and dedication
in their selfless preservation

from one generation to the next)

but to continue,
the carney men and women of yore
might be dead and gone now
but they have been replaced
with a new breed of huckster
spieler, pitchman and woman

it's just a new
more improved spiel
by a newer and more improved
repackaged carney man,
barker and petty con-artist

dressed in an expensive
three piece suit
(or pantsuit)
only now he or she
comes to us

with an Ivy League pedigree
barking, spieling and spewing out
the same old shit

clothed and smartly wrapped neatly
in the false garb
of "change" and "fundamental transformation"

wherein I hear
the same ole, same ole
cleverly and unctuously
sloughed and palmed off as

"change that we must have"

that we
absolutely, positively need
or surely we shall all die

and thusly I hear these pitchmen and women
these oily, lubricious, imperious hucksters
these con men and women
sing their siren song

of a free lunch
for everyone
with their endless empty promises
of a lot of something
for a lot of nothing

with their
Marxist class warfare
oaths to soak the rich
and tax those evil critters
into oblivion

for to be rich
and productive
and successful
for such as these
is truly evil

so tax
the rich into la-la-land
they clamor
and spread the wealth around
they say self-righteously

and I say
go ahead,

dine sumptuously
on the fatted calf just like kings and princes
in this glorious moment of yours
in your splendid, evanescent "here and now"

cause when your princely feast
is done
there ain't never gonna be
another fatted calf ever again

and likewise I assure you
dear readers
it ain't mere pocket, chomp change

these modern day
spielers and hucksters
aim their grubby, greedy paws
and rapacious paunches at

so that we now stand at a crossroads
and a precipitous precipice
of our own making
viewing a present
populated by up and coming
boomers and yuppies

and a future
of generations
of slackers and gen-X-ers
of hosts and legions of even softer
more stultified and under-educated millennials

of these overly propagandized and proselytized
lemming-like
unthinking, uncritical, un-analytical

mindlessly conformist
automatons and robots
and mind-numbed zombies

spieling and huckstering
their college and university
professors'
trite and thin-worn
socialist dribble and warmed over Marxist spittle
in unanimous group think

like a troop of
trained barking and honking seals
clapping happily and eagerly
to the steady downbeat drumbeat

of their yabbering, blathering vindictive Machiavellian deity
Saul Alinsky-ite vermin
with their New Age, Marcusian, Chomski-ite
Neo-Marxist doggerel and imbecilic prattle

is this,
will it be,
their so very meager
patrimony and legacy left to us
by the Greatest generation ever?

these boomers
these slackers and gen-X-ers
these lilliputians
these legions and armies of empty suits and empty minds?

To all those brave and hardy
generations before them
in the continuum of American

greatness and Exceptionalism

what do we have to look forward to?
save for a nation of whiners and malcontents
in a cacophonous babble
of Balkanized, vested special-interest groups

bickering, nipping and barking at each other's heels
with insatiable appetites and demands
and mindless whims and caprices

fashionably spouting multi-cultural doggerel
and plying their
anti-intellectual freedom
and anti-inalienable human and civil rights
pure, unadulterated fascism

under the banner of self-righteous
self-serving
philosophically and morally indefensible
political correctness

so again, what will our future be
but one
populated by hosts and legions
of these luddite liberals and 'commie-lib' fascists?

these mindless naysayers
who say 'no' to everything,
'no' to American greatness,
self-reliance and rugged individualism

and 'no' to the frontier spirit
of our forbears
and 'no' to our pioneering ethos

and legacy

and 'no'
to the heritage of American Christianity
with its Protestant Natural Law
and its divine gift of
American Exceptionalism

and even 'no'
to our triumph over terrorism
and 'no' even to our own self-defense
and our very own self-preservation

are these
leftist lilliputians
these spoiled, pampered
miserable ingrates

our ultimate
legacy and patrimony
to ourselves
and to the rest of the world?

for if they are
then woe unto us
and woe unto the world

for surely
there will be no tomorrow
worth having,
nor hope nor virtue
for us and the rest of humanity

for I surely dread such a happenstance
for surely a world

without a great and Exceptional America
will surely be a dark and dreary,
truly dreadfully barbaric and deadly place

Chapter IX
Yet More Sorrowful and Lamentable Professions
of Buyer's Remorseful Confessions

So irony of ironies
the Greatest Generation ever
was not all that perfect
after all

for lamentably they birthed
and gave rise
to generations of a lesser mettle
with a thin and tenuous character
of a baser metal than themselves

who in turn gave rise
to an internal
utterly insidious
evil
from within

and to paraphrase
Will Durant
the great American encyclopediast,

scholar, historian and philosopher

(I paraphrase here
cause I can't quote anyone
to save my life
besides which
I'm too damn lazy to look it up)

"a great civilization is not destroyed
from without
until it has destroyed
and conquered itself from within"

and might I add
with moral rot and decay
corruption and decadence
and a failure of the will

to defend either its culture
or its civic institutions
and ultimately its very own essence and existence
from both within and without

and so the Greatest Generation ever
allowed itself to be duped and mesmerized,
and unbeknownst to itself,
corrupted and ultimately overrun

by a truly perfidious enemy
of liberal-leftist, counter-culture
quislings and fifth columnists
from within

you know, of course dear readers
of whom I speak

that infamous gang
of the usual, insidious suspects:

the liberal politicos and bleeding-heart
co-conspiratorial pundits
with their long skein
of liberal qua commie-lib qua commie
qua Marxist dévotees and mindless,
'group think' zombified acolytes

and of course
the Hollywood Left and the pop culture
populated by an even more
vacuous and brain dead assortment
of lefty, pinkos

and then of course
the commanding heights
of the high culture
and the cloacal, sewer-bound putrid depths
of the low culture too

and of course
the entire liberal, media-elite
as well as the mostly Marxist, professorial
Panglossian hypocrites of the Cloud Cuckoo-land
insane domain of our colleges and universities

and then of course
the anti-American, anti-Christian ACLU
the far leftist second coming
and inheritors of the Grand Inquisition,
and the lesser inheritors of the Gestapo and the KGB
and other thought-police sophists throughout the ages

and of course
the multicultural frauds and charlatans
and diversity witch hunters and pimps,
and the rabid homosexual, sordid and perverse
sexual predators and pederasts, as well as
the diesel dyke femmee-Nazis too

all these thought-police storm troopers
so very thoroughly steeped
in intellectual, philosophic and ideological
fascistic 'political correctness'

and a whole bunch of other
simultaneously risible Thyrsetes
and damnably, downright
evil Iagos and Uriah Heaps,
truly in effect, evil personified

and all of them
communitarian, instrumentalist, obscurantist
moral relativist, social-scientific determinist
liberal-progressive, leftist, Marxist villains

all so very devious and deceptive
and all of them
so very intellectually, spiritually, morally and philosophically
moronic, imbecilic, idiotic and cretinous
and quite sadly and lamentably
all too numerous to mention

and so that is my
very small 'short list'
of the damnable
destroyers of America
from within

and I assure you dear readers
what makes all this so sad,
forlorn and hopeless
is that it is truly a very short list

but irony of ironies
most of these instrumentalist
and social-scientific determinists
and moral relativist villains
supposedly all have good intentions

for they truly believe,
as 'true believers' always do,
that they have both God and ultimate reason,
truth and justice on their side,

and so therefore, they justify and reason to themselves
that they must logically needs be
have an absolute vise-grip
stranglehold Cartel-like, monopoly on all of the former,

and if not God,
certainly reason and irreversible,
incontrovertible absolute truth

(but again ironically,
they are predominantly, almost exclusively
all godless, extreme secularists and atheists

who neither believe in religion
nor the existence of God
in the first place
and oh how deliciously ironic
that be)

and so the poets
have got this one
ever so right
when they sing
so very accurately

that the very path to hell
is oft so thoroughly paved
with the mortar, tar and bricks
of good intentions,
just causes and so-called supposed
noble goals and ends

and so the Greatest Generation ever
allowed itself
to be mesmerized, hoodwinked and duped
by liberalism and progressivism
with their many false Gods and empty promises

for they truly hungered for those
feel-good, do-good,
insincere and feckless Rooseveltian
socialist panaceas and elixirs, bromides and nostrums

and like those rubes and suckers,
they too had fallen prey to the slick
carney men and women
at the big top and little tent

just I as a mere child had marveled
sixty-four years ago
as an awestruck five year old
so very mesmerized
by those very clever and cunning
carney barkers, spielers, pitchmen and women

for I too had been hypnotized
by their bright lights
and their false promises
and by their specious arguments
and glib sales pitches

with their craven images
of ersatz gods and goddesses
with visions of sugar plums and dollar bills
falling like manna from the very heavens themselves
from their secular nirvanas
and their utopian workers' paradises here on earth

and likewise my elders,
that Greatest Generation ever,
had also easily succumbed
and listened intently

to those very intent,
liberal bullshit artists
weave and spin their bullshit
so cleverly and appealingly
so adroitly and persuasively
and all so lubriciously and unctuously

and they too
like fish in a barrel
had bought the liberal spiel,
hook, line and sinker
ever so gleefully and gullibly

for those liberal
pols and pundits
promised them this universe and beyond
and the psychobabblers preached

their psychobabble

and the moral relativists
and social-scientific determinists
and the logical positivists
preached their "Iron Triangle of Amorality"

and the communitarians and instrumentalists
and the usual suspect liberals qua progressives
qua liberal socialists qua socialists qua scientific socialists
qua communists qua Marxists
all preached their deceits and lies

and a vast disparate, cacophonous
counter-culture arose
led by intellectually dangerous
Marxist-elitist clowns
at the head of vast armies of student barbarians

who preached their mindless, mind-numbed
group think anarchy and chaos
and politically correct conformity
and dystopian violence

those hosts and legions
of leftist charlatans and frauds
who so smartly and persuasively
chanted their mantra, siren song of

"down is up,
and up is down"

and who then declared
"treason is more honorable
than military service,

and desertion and dodging the draft
is the highest form of patriotism,"
truly their highest calling

and "appeasement of our enemies
and aiding and abetting them
and stabbing our allies in the back"
somehow is also the highest form of patriotism too

for treason, appeasement and desertion
somehow they reasoned
(and still do to this very day)
are the noblest forms of dissent

and so the libs qua commie libs
qua lefty-pinko Marxists
hid behind their phony dissent
and thoroughly perverted the First Amendment
with the aid and 'useful idiot' complicity
of the very liberal, Warren Supreme Court

and then of course,
the Washington post and the New York Times
vied and competed with each other
to see who could best, first and fastest,
reveal vital state secrets
prominently upon their front pages

and thereby
thwart our national security and compromise our foreign policy
and even endanger our own secret agents
and our soldiers on the field of battle
as well as our agents of diplomacy

and again

all these usual suspects
declared quite coyly

"down is up, and up is down"

and indeed they ushered in an age
of true Orwellian proportions and dimensions
of "New Speak" and "Double Speak"
couched in terms of politically correct fascism

and these liberal-leftist fascists
added to their fascistic repertoire
with multi-cultural doggerel
and with speech codes too
and phony diversity dogma
and divisive, racial preferences and set-asides

and many of the Greatest Generation ever
again, much too many of them
bought their spiel
wholly and gullibly
and especially that
of the voodoo, witch-doctor psychobabblers too

and that of their patron saints
of child rearing
of their anointed, be-knighted, holy saints
Doctor Spock and Madame Montessori
and also with the Johnny-come-lately Dr. Hazleton interloper too

who preached and taught them
to spare the rod
and wholly embrace permissiveness
and unearned, phony self-esteem
and to love and talk the little tykes into submission

who in turn
made good parents
into bad parents
and in the process
ruined one generation after another

but why?
how could this possibly be?
how could the Greatest Generation ever
have been so damn gullible?

how could they buy
this constant, endless parade
of liberal-lefty sham and flim-flam men and women
with their utterly deceitful hucksterism?

for you see dear readers
for many
these issues
were just simply
much too esoteric

for indeed
the Greatest Generation ever
was just simply much too busy in pursing and ensuring
its own future and that of its children and grandchildren
for indeed they were just simply too damn busy
in building the Greatest nation ever

but for many
if not most
the great poverty and suffering
of the Great Depression
and the savage vicissitudes of World War II

were still so very recent and fresh
in both their minds and hearts
and were so very indelibly seared
in their flesh and into the very innermost
recesses and depths of their very souls

and along came these
smooth con men and women
these liberal-elite hucksters, barkers and spielers
preaching a whole lot of something for a whole lot of nothing

who slyly inveigled and deceived
the Greatest Generation ever,
those men and women
who had endured the Great Depression

and who had triumphed over
the utter evil of Nazism
of fascism and Japanese imperialism

and who had triumphed
over naked aggression
and ruthless and remorseless armed conquest
and armed subversion throughout the world

and ultimately won the Cold War
and defeated the former Soviet Union
arguably the very worst
feudal-socialist, totalitarian state
in all of recorded history

(with the possible exception
of Maoist China)

who sadly somehow

allowed themselves to be swayed
by their fond memories
of FDR and his cult of personality,
their liberal-progressive savior

whom they admired
beyond the coronation of royalty
and in essence esteemed
beyond the boundaries of
godlike adoration and adulation

for they indeed
raised him to the very heavens
in an apotheosis and deification of him
worthy of and equal to that of
a Caesar or an Augustus,
or to that of a mad Caligula or an insane Nero

and so the Greatest Generation ever
blinded by their own indifference and apathy,
for again
most were just simply too damn busy
building the greatest nation ever

or in many cases
were themselves so very blinded
by their very own false rhetoric
and insidious propaganda

for even the Greatest Generation ever
had its very own share of leftist traitors and quislings
amongst them, those residual lefty-pinko
agitators and community organizers
from the 20s, 30s and 40s
and of course again

their own progeny of usual suspects
with their even more effective
aforementioned evil chicanery

in their embrace
of their ersatz gods of liberal socialism
and their darker demons
of communism and Marxism

for again for the umpteenth time,
the Greatest Generation ever
was just too damn busy
to pay much attention

to this growing, creeping, crawling
cancer of overweening
anti-American, anti-Christian
secular progressivism and liberal socialism and beyond

or to the remorseless growing creation
of ingrained social dysfunction and social pathology
and its insane and lunatic glorification
by a culture run amok and gone berserk
thoroughly infected with the mental disease and disorder
of liberalism and socialism, communism and Marxism

all serenaded
by an antistrophic Greek chorus
of psychobabbler quacks and hacks
spewing their endless pseudo-scientific
oft, nay, mostly politically correct
charlatan panaceas, fraudulent diseases and disorders
with their phony, anti-common sense nostrums and cures

and so the Greatest Generation ever

succumbed to this
at first
imperceptible onslaught

for it surely and truly was
the proverbial, invidious and insidious death
by ten thousand, tiny and barely perceptible
cuts and blows
ever so innocuously felt or realized

but this steady and persistent trickle
then became a stream
and that stream a raging mighty river
and that swelling river, a deluge

which has now become
a mighty torrent
of collectivist, statism and socialism
and politically correct, intolerant anti-Americanism
and anti-Christian secularism and atheism

all while
the usual suspect, demonic clowns
wrought upon us
their massive evil and their dastardly deceits
and insidious, dirty lies and tricks

so that all these usual suspects
have thoroughly worked and weaved
so very adroitly and skillfully

their truly nefarious, vile dirty work
into the consciousness
and very moral fiber and fabric
of the tapestry of America

upon both the body politic
and deep within our very own souls
hearts and minds

and have wreaked havoc
and social dysfunction,
social pathology and dystopian, social disintegration
wherever they have dared to tread

and have laid waste
and coarsened our culture,
contaminated and polluted it
and all so furtively and perniciously

and all so freely, libertinely and licentiously
and all so promiscuously and gratuitously
and all from within

and so again
we now stand forlornly
at the crossroads
of our very own existence

naked to the world
bereft and shorn
of our once upon a time
not so very long ago,

many national, manly virtues
and defiant will to succeed and triumph
and ultimately
to exist freely and independently

and if we do succumb

it will solely be due
to the utter rot and decay
from within

from that list
of usual suspects
of insane, irrational
wild men from Borneo

liberal-lefty pinko
freaks and geeks
in upscale, tony designer-jeans
and three piece suits

with fancy college degrees
and Ivy League pedigrees
always ever still eternally
spouting communist dribble
and warmed over Marxist spittle

is this our future
our fate and ignominious destiny?
these legions of clever and cunning
yuppies and geriatric baby boomers

and their progeny of slackers
and gen-X-ers and millennials
more spoiled rotten and pampered
self-serving and sophistic,
self-centered and hedonistic

than any generation
ever before them
to have ever tread upon this land
this earth of ours

is this
all there is?
just a bunch of glib, empty suits
who talk a good game

and articulate
their utter nihilism
and secular, moral relativism
and liberal-leftist dogmatic theology

all so damn
persuasively
and all so
adroitly and self-righteously?

Chapter X
And Finally Some Last Rites and Other Pronouncements

And so alas
the beat goes on
in the middle of this
post-modernist, deconstructionist Midway

where the neon, pinball
electric light-show of the past
with its cacophonous acid-rock noise
and primitive ear-splitting heavy-metal vibes

has now been replaced by a LED
oh so sophisticated laser-lit runway
of mindless 'grunge' screechings
and bad boy 'hip-hop'
senseless, vile, mindless scratchings

where now,
these modern day 'rock 'n rollers'
sing and serenade
their secularist mentors and allies

with their siren songs
of failed socialism
in strophic and antistrophic syncopation,
as a chorus in Greek tragedy

and they sing these,
their paeans of praise and deception
in a somnambulant lullaby
of not so subtle persuasion and indoctrination

and these newest, New Age
rock 'n rollers
of the newest, latest rendition
of the once Mighty Midway

sing their instrumentalist songs
of moral relativism
and Marxist dribble
ever so mindlessly and ever so eternally

Oh hear Ye
all Ye faithful
hear these
my former

spaced out acid-rock
and juiced up, drug drenched
hopped up heavy-metal vibes
in electrified, rarified, mystical Muzak

and hear Ye now
their current 'grunge' maddened ravings
and bad boy 'hip-hop' mindless refrains
in an utter dissonant, discordant, cacophonous symphony

Oh hear Ye
this very last ultimate
Orwellian reprieve
of theirs

for now a very mighty
transcendental, karmic metaphysics
has evolved
and emerged

and they chant in conformist solidarity
"right is Wrong
and wrong is Right
and good is Evil
and evil is Good"

and so I must
now conclude
that the future portends
oh so very ominously

for the barbarians
are no longer
at the gates
but are deep within them

and as I see it
there ain't no future
worth having
with these worthless sort about

and so I must
sadly and forlornly
bid adieu
to the once Mighty Midway

and to the dream and promise
and last best hope
of all of humankind
throughout time immemorial

that was once
upon a time
not so very long ago

America

the bold, the brave
the truly altruistic
Exceptionalist experiment

and yet with all its flaws and excesses
still God's gift to humanity
still the very last best hope of humankind
still that shining city upon a hill

still the beacon of freedom
and of inalienable, God given human and civil rights
still the torchbearer and pioneer
of liberal, democratic, enlightened capitalism

still the leader and standard bearer
of human progress and civilization
and of the rights of man
of life, liberty and the pursuit of happiness

for surely the world will be
a much lesser place
and the human race
so very much more diminished
without an America

for surely this world without an America
this globe, this little planet of ours
will be a much darker, deadlier place
one so very much more savage and barbaric,
dangerous and evil than it has ever been

for surely such a state of affairs
will be the end of times
and the end of human progress
and of civilization as we know it

for surely such a calamity
and worldwide catastrophe
shall usher in
a New Dark Age

one so much more sinister and evil
than any other ever experienced,
suffered and endured,
in the vast annals of time immemorial

and sadly and dolefully so
I lament and rue such an event
and bitterly weep in my heart and soul
the coming of that horrible, infamous, ignoble day

and as the
Roman poet Vergil
once declaimed lamentably
"Danaos dona ferentes timeo"
literally "I fear Greeks bearing gifts"

so I too likewise fear
with great trepidation
apprehension and loathing

the coming of these
Brave New World generations
of boomers, slackers, yuppies, millennials and gen-X-ers
and their offspring yet to be born

these Neo-Marxist automatons
these brain-dead moral relativists and brainwashed
proselytized, robotized, uncritical, unthinking
highly conformist, solipsistic, hedonistic, narcissistic
Neo-Marxist zombies

so thoroughly indoctrinated in
and stupefied by,
their very own communist dribble
and warmed over Marxist spittle

surely such a world
shall be a lesser, darker place
one in which the human race

and all of humanity
shall wholly suffer unholy,
ineffable horrors
and a fate wholly unthinkable and unspeakable

and so I pray
unto God and my fellow man
to save and spare us
from such a horrid fate and destiny

but I must also finally ask
is it inevitable?
or do we have
a choice?

is there any possibility at all,
any chance no matter how slight it might be
to survive this grim,
very grim future of ours?

but these questions
unfortunately for me
are all well beyond my ken,
and or ability and power to determine or alter,
and ultimately,
beyond the final limits of my own
fast approaching mortality

for my day
has surely
come and gone
and for better or worse
has all but weaved its full course

for surely
tis nigh time's evening's
high tide for me

as Charon relentlessly guides
my destiny's ship remorselessly
upon the River Styx
as I go to meet
my final, ineluctable, fated last journey

So I,
at long last,
bid you,
dear readers,
a very final, most ultimate, fond Adieu

CPSIA information can be obtained
at www.ICGtesting.com
Printed in the USA
BVHW042019240422
635205BV00012B/427